Bending the Rules

Angela Pritchard

Bending the Rules

Bending the Rules
ISBN 978 1 76109 250 3
Copyright © text Angela Pritchard 2022
Cover image: Angela Pritchard

First published 2022 by
GINNINDERRA PRESS
PO Box 3461 Port Adelaide 5015
www.ginninderrapress.com.au

You're somewhere in my house. An insect. A cricketty creature whose chirping is a constant sound, or are you rubbing your wings together? When the singing stops, I forget about you. Till I see you, unmoving, silent in the unused bath. And an uncanny thing happens. Over the next days, I am to receive a message from a creature so small that finally I bury you in a matchbox with a bright flower to mark the place.

Now, however, I consider how I can end your life as quickly and as painlessly as possible.

Step into the bath and crush you underfoot? No.

Insecticide? Worse. A slow and unpleasant death.

I leave you there.

The next day, I look down at you and wonder if you are dead. The following day when I peer into the bathtub I think, well, now I do believe that you have died.

You wave one long feeler at me. After that salute, I cannot move you, but in some way I believe you have no pain.

I see you several times every day and contemplate nothing more than your being. Alive? I can no longer tell, and I am not privileged to know when you do take your last breath.

I think of my own being, my biblical three score years and ten, and am suddenly aware that you are showing me that dying is a simple and acceptable part of your life. Did you come to perform a task you knew was ahead of you? To experience the peaceful end of a cricketty life in a warm space?

Eventually, one morning, I do lift you carefully into your small coffin and strangely, because of you, I remember the last night of my beloved father's life.

I can see him now. As I sit beside his nursing home bed, briefly he lifts his hand from where it lies upon the bedcover and turns it palm upward spreading his fingers. A gesture encompassing this last night together, as he says his final words.

Touch is gone in an instant. Words can last for ever. Father, you coloured my life, hugged me with words, used with wisdom from within your one-time six-foot frame, Daddy, the title sometimes seen to be pretentious, who became Dad, and finally, in your last years, my beloved Rupert. I thank you, and with greed I steal back fragments of memories now, in an attempt to fit together the jigsaw pieces of our lives.

*

At three or four years of age, I thought my father was perfect. It's possible that he thought the same about me. Later in life, I learned more about the word 'love', and to question the many distortions of perfection within it.

In our garden in England, near to London, my sister and I dig a hole and begin to shore up a tunnel. We know without doubt that our excavations will finish up in Australia. Then, to our dismay, someone tells us that the centre of the earth is red with fire and burning hot. Two solemn little girls consult their father with this problem.

'When you do get to the centre, I shall buy each of you a fireproof suit,' is his equally earnest but exciting response.

Now, here in Perth, I hear the happy chatter of small children several gardens away and smile at the thought that they may be digging their way to England. If so, I expect their tunnels, too, will collapse in a very short time.

Many years later, I recalled one special evening, and wrote this free verse poem full of memories.

> I remember damp November air, smell again coalfire smoke from chimneys.
> Two solemn children watch Father,

our hero of Guy Fawkes night,
move from place to place in the garden setting up a frieze of fireworks.
As darkness falls small fingers within home-made woollen mittens,
orange this year,
juggle potatoes, too hot
with their nothing-special floury smell and oven-charred skins.
On the uneven brick path proud rockets stand in empty sauce bottles
and jam jars,
awaiting life from a lighted match.
A cluster of Catherine wheels
nailed to wooden fence posts,
promise to revolve without juddering disappointment.
I remember, at last Father moves to ignite his display
the sombre sky frothing with showers of light,
to fall on apple trees and lawn.
Fountains of gold whoosh upwards illuminating the lilac bush
beneath which tortoises sleep buried under leaves.
Wheels spin obediently leaving tails of brightness,
revealing Father's gentle smile,
and small eyes shine.
From behind steamed windowpanes Mother, baby on her hip, watches,
with a slight 'for richer or poorer, till death us do part' Charleston shimmy.
She knows
peace on earth once more.
The wetness, the shine in her eyes, is a grown up one.

Another evening Dad says, 'Upstairs and into bed now, I'll be up soon to read you a story.'

I run. My sister follows much more slowly. We know he has to finish his cigarette. In our side-by-side beds, we settle down to wait. This is a good night. Daddy is home.

As usual, he sits on the low chair under the sloping ceiling. The two beds are close together in the small room, but it is hard to hear the story. Why does my sister's breathing have to be so noisy? I'm tired of her always being unwell. It's not much fun having a sister if she can't run and play much. I pull the blankets right up under my chin and concentrate on listening.

Another noise is building at this time, an ambulance ranging the quiet streets. I think of it now as a siren blaring, but maybe in those war years a shrill bell. Nearer and nearer, louder and louder, until suddenly it stops. It must be right outside our house.

'Come, my dear.' Our father stands abruptly and drops the book. With care, he picks up my small sister from the other bed and carries her out of the room.

I cannot believe it. The book lies open on the chair, the story unfinished. Tears of anger come to my eyes, and I bang my fists under the blankets. 'She gets all the attention,' I mutter. 'It's not fair.'

How do I see this now? My father reading a story to create a semblance of normality. Probably for himself as much as for us. Listening, listening for the ambulance he has requested, having, as a physician at the nearby outer London hospital, a telephone by his bed. Asked too to have an oxygen tent in readiness for his daughter. And I see too my mother downstairs with her head in her hands.

My sister had many severe asthma attacks in wintertime but eventually they became less and less severe, and she grew strong.

We had three tortoises as pets. It was explained to us that they led interesting lives, and didn't have fur, as did dogs and cats, to cause asthma. In summer, they chomped happily with blunt mouths on mother's herbaceous border plants, and absolutely loved fruit. The smallest one trundled around with most of its head inside a Victoria plum for a little while till it was lovingly extricated. Being put to bed in doll's prams was tolerated as were trips in bicycle baskets, but for the winter months, of course, they hibernated. We left our three little pets to sleep under big piles of leaves in a box in the sunroom, and impatiently waited for spring to come. Watching the little creatures waken slowly to warmth delighted us each year.

I don't know which year our family acquired a car. I do remember that it was grey, and that finally something inhabited the garage.

Before this new toy, my dad had set off to the local hospital on a bicycle. The legs of his flapping grey trousers were held by metal clips to prevent the bicycle chain leaving dark black grease marks on them. I imagine that during this time we girls had not visited his place of work. With a car in the family, my sister and I were allowed to accompany him occasionally and amuse ourselves in the sprawling hospital grounds. What a help this must have been for our busy mother.

On one occasion, we played near a large pond. We paddled at the water's edge. We laughed. We splashed each other. And we absolutely infuriated a pair of large white swans with a nest nearby. The noise these hissing thrashing creatures made as they attacked us, and our own squawks of terror, alerted several people who hurried to protect us.

Looking back, I see, in the middle of this group, the doctor with whom we had breakfast every morning, waving his arms wildly and running, as his white coat flapped around his legs.

It had a happy ending. We were rescued.

The advent of the car also meant that on some days en route to a park to climb trees, we two older girls had another adventure. Outside a large building, we were carefully locked in the car with the stern words, 'Do not open the windows. Do not get out of the car. Not for any reason at all.'

Father then went off to do his medical rounds at what I now believe was an institution for criminals found to be, in the word of the era, insane.

While he is gone, we giggle on the back seat. We poke each other and try to make our faces look mad enough to get us locked up in the big brick building, where our father will visit us from time to time.

*

One morning, which I now realise would probably have been Anzac

Day in April, he gathered my sister and me from our play onto the upstairs landing of our house. We stood looking up at him as he told us through tears of memory how his father had gone to the First World War and not returned. He had been thirteen years old and his brother fifteen at the time.

My father and his brother were born and grew up in Maryborough in Australia. Their father was a doctor at the hospital there, and had volunteered for the Australian Medical Corps after war broke out. He died in Egypt in 1917 of a severe kidney infection. His two boys later qualified as doctors in Australia, and travelled to England in the 1930s with their mother for further studies. My father was to become a Member of the Royal College of Physicians, and my uncle a Fellow of the Royal College of Surgeons. How proud my grandmother would have been of her sons. Both married in England and started their families there.

Now in outer London, our dad, as dependable as the roof over our heads in our two-storey semi-detached home, added his own magic. He turned big wooden boxes into houses where we kept the privet hawk caterpillars we hunted for in the hedge in our front garden. They were big lime-green creatures with what looked like large painted eyes. We fed them on the privet leaves till they turned into chrysalises and then, in the circle of life, into the large moths we set free to fly away.

To wake in the morning to find the bedroom strangely light and the street below almost silent meant the excitement of snow overnight. When we crept down the carpeted stairs and opened the back door, whiteness was everywhere, but not only snow. Dad had put his photographic trays full of water onto the lawn, and we had ice blocks to play with too.

However, if my childhood was enhanced by his presence, I look back and see my mother doing what she did best. Mothering. Warmth. Meals. Listening. These were her incomparable gifts to her offspring, her only complaint being that she would like to have been given another pair of hands.

Stairs and banisters were part of life too. I recall evenings over years which would have been late in the war or post-war, sneaking with my sister from our beds to watch parties down below. With apples from trees in the small garden my parents brewed home-made wine which appeared to be the cause of much laughter from friends, colleagues and their partners.

What a wonderful achievement, though. To give small children a safe, nurtured childhood as a war raged throughout the world. News, however, was not as frequent or as easy to access as it can be today.

We recited,

> Thank you for the world so sweet
> Thank you for the food we eat
> Thank you for the birds that sing
> Thank you God for everything.

And we believed. Our world, the small one around us, was a sweet one.

But there were rules to be learned too.

*

My mother was my father's complimentary colour, his soulmate, and the love of his life. She had been the sister-in-charge on his medical ward. If she was the other half of his wholeness, she was as well in some ways his shadow, deferring to him, and looking up to him, often with gratitude, There was also the role-playing element of the era. They were in their mid-thirties when they married. 'I had to teach him how to kiss,' she told me in my adult life. She also said that he told her he was looking for a wife with long hair, who had a thousand pounds in the bank, and was still a virgin. 'Two out of three wasn't bad, was it?' she added with a laugh. I never asked her whether she had long hair when they first met.

I don't believe I was conceived on a bar stool, but I think it may not have been far away from one. On Saint Valentine's Day 1939. I worked it out.

Germany invaded Poland on the first of September that same year. Two days later, the people of England gathered around wireless sets to hear their prime minister, Neville Chamberlain, broadcast to the nation from 10 Downing Street.

> This morning the British Ambassador in Berlin handed the German government a final note stating that unless we heard from them by 11 o'clock that they were prepared at once to withdraw their troops from Poland, a state of war would exist between us. I have to tell you now that no such undertaking has been received, and consequently, this country is at war with Germany.

Insecurity? Fear? Anxiety? I cannot imagine the emotions elicited. My mother was seven months pregnant.

A November baby that same year. A Scorpio, and also a war baby, whose first word was 'bomber'. 'Fighter' was, I imagine, more difficult at the age of two.

Do I look back, though, and feel that I was almost privileged? Growing up in a city where people were giving their metal front gates for the making of weapons. Where tiny pink flowers of London pride began quietly to show themselves on bomb sites.

My gorgeous mother, who loved me first then my two sisters, never ever letting us think that she would have liked a boy. No. We girls knew we were specially ordered. She was a state registered nurse and midwife when, before antibiotics, nursing involved long arduous hours, but she never worked again after her marriage.

I try to imagine being my mother in those years. I see her thin body huddled within the warm woollen coat. A cotton scarf is tied under her chin. I shiver as in my mind I see the pensive expression on her face as she gathers my small sister to her and holds my hand tight.

It is 1945. We stand in line with other women and children. We wait. The war in Europe is over and the world holds its breath as the concept of 'peace once more' is grasped. What we wait for is not sinister or frightening. Homes have no refrigerators, so we wait to buy fresh food.

Much of London is in ruins, and I imagine now the quiet relief my mother feels as she stands in that street, that our suburb has been spared. Vaguely, I recall nights spent underground in a bomb shelter, and remember being carried there half asleep in my father's arms. The smell of damp soil returns in my mind, and I see again the woodlice we called slaters, on the corrugated-tin walls. I was not aware that coal for heating was rationed to two tons a year for the average family home, or that street lighting, which for so long had been nil, was still reduced. We did not go out on the street at night. I was not aware that the pastures of England lay unproductive because farm workers had been fighting for our country. Food was in shorter supply that year than at any time during the war. There were many hardships I was not conscious of.

In my mind, I see my mother reach up to brush the hair from her face and pull her scarf tighter. There is a cold wind blowing. My sister and I are serious children and we stand quietly next to her on the pavement in our neat home-made coats. I imagine the distraction she feels as she plans meals for the week ahead. I try to comprehend her hopelessness in queuing for food to feed a family, with the shortage of fruit, meat and eggs for growing children. Also I realise now that she was pregnant again.

My mother was a child through the previous war, and a teenager through the depression years. In the late 1920s she was groomed, as were many of her contemporaries, to be a 'lady'. Gloves and hats were important items of clothing, and if she was to marry well, she must know how to cook delectable meals. She learnt to bake cakes and biscuits, to prepare fowl for the oven and to glaze a ham. Part of the art of being a good cook was in the presentation, and always with a beautiful table setting. With all the hope of being an acceptably accomplished wife, my mother married her much-loved man.

How shattering it must have been to find themselves caring for small children while a war raged across half the world. They were not alone, and my mind returns to us queuing patiently for food with other residents of our outer London suburb.

Ration cards made each family's quota of food fair, but often the content was not very appealing.

If my mother was lucky, there would be a rabbit or some liver. These would be treats, although sometimes tough and a little unpalatable.

Often there was only a piece of mutton. This would make a hot meal, then a cold meal, and then, minced with the addition of bread, would become rissoles. My sister and I obtained a liking for tripe as children. Our mother cooked it in sauce with onions grown on the small portion of land allocated to my father by the local shire to grow vegetables. She also did interesting things with ox hearts, with sweetbreads, and with dripping from the meat. Cakes and scones were achieved using powdered eggs and milk. There was also a remarkable meal called Leftovers.

All this she achieved with dignity, good humour and, always, a beautifully set table. My mother was, as were many other strong women of her time, a versatile and extraordinarily good cook.

*

Many years later, I began writing short stories and poems. This poem, reflecting on the war years in London, I entered for a competition, where it was deemed clichéd.

I have, however, always liked it.

Christmas Day, London, 1945

> A peaceful Christmas morning,
> wintry English dawning,
> and quiet fragile reverence
> descends on London's streets.
>
> Lights are on, the blackout gone,
> harsh war no more a fear.
> Fragments of a carol drift,
> a child's voice sweet and clear.
>
> Parents share a silent prayer
> for grieving families everywhere,
> while children do not understand
> and clamour for their treats.

Gifts once more beneath the tree,
but now the difference
is peace, more precious on this day
than myrrh or frankincense.

London wakes and London aches
for losses during war,
but proud unwavering church bells ring,
as peace is hers once more.

*

At eleven years of age, I was enrolled to attend an all-girls high school in London. It involved travelling back and forth every day by train.

I was growing up in outer London. I liked it. Streets with houses crowded together all full of people. Living in such an area meant being in close proximity to many citizens of different ages, backgrounds and gender. I have always been a little wary of open spaces. I like light switches and gas heaters, and I would not choose to run away to the countryside because of something unpleasant that happened to me when I was eleven years old.

*

A few years later, a diary entry might have read,

> Today is a horrible day. Dad is angry with me. He says I have no right to take money for my bus fare to swimming and then borrow a bicycle without telling him. He says it's deceitful. He says he expects more of me, and now I feel like a thief.

Swimming this afternoon, and I borrow Anne's bike from the school bike shed as usual. After all, we're good friends and tennis partners. We practise together in every lunch break. I'm peddling down the hill and through the main road traffic to Wandsworth and all is okay. Our swimming lesson at the baths there is as lovely as ever. On the way back, I stop in the high street and prop the bike up against the kerb using the pedal, because there's a jumper in a shop window I had noticed.

Suddenly I hear a crash, a bang, car noises, and shouting. Anne's bicycle has blown down into the street, and a red double-decker bus has run over most of it. People are stopping to look as the bus driver slowly backs off.

I don't know what to do. I stand looking at the disaster on the road and feel a little sick. Someone lifts it onto the pavement and the bus moves slowly on. A lady stops to talk with me. She says she'll stay till the policeman who is on his way comes. I feel stupid in my school uniform. I can't even park a bike correctly, but I do have my school bag.

A policeman does arrive. He's about as old as Dad, and he's so kind about what has happened to me that I start to cry. We walk together to the police station and he carries the crumpled bicycle. I have to sit and wait while he writes a report about it all, and I rummage through my bag for a hanky to blow my nose. I'm wondering what Anne is going to say to me.

I have to get a bus back to school but I do have the threepence I was trying to save anyway.

I'm very late back to the school grounds and Anne is the only one there, waiting around for her bike to go home. I tell her what happened and she's kind about it all but we don't talk much. Neither of us knows what will ensue from this incident, and she sets off to walk to her house.

When I finally arrive at home, I am still a mess of tears as I pour the story out to Mum.

She is really kind about it all too and tells me she's just happy that I'm not hurt. 'Don't worry, darling, when Dad gets home he'll sort it out,' she says.

I look back at this event in the summer before my fifteenth birthday and realise things that I didn't see then. I like to think that now I would be the adult who stayed with a teenager in trouble, and I hope I thanked her.

Also the comprehension that two parents are still separate individual people. Sometimes black and white, sometimes a little grey in their response to events within family life. Maybe there is also a slight gender response within it all. I wonder now how my parents talked together about that day later in the evening. My mother so concerned for me and Dad so moralistic about the money.

I think for me it ended there. My father did buy a new bicycle for my friend Anne. I guess he was expected to. I don't remember that the whole episode was ever mentioned again, but it has stayed in my memory.

Anne left school less than a year later and I didn't see her again.

School days, and weeks, and months went on and I did enjoy them but at the end of our upper fifth year when I was sixteen, I told my parents I wanted to leave and train to be a nurse. 'No, no, no,' was their almost synchronised response. 'Hard work. Poorly paid. Think about it, dear. Please, stay at school another two years.'

To keep them happy, I remained at school for another two years, and have never regretted it. I studied hard, became a prefect, and played tennis for the school. During that time, I was impressed by other girls who indulged in activities I had never given any thought to. They went to shops where they stole lipsticks while they pretended to decide which nylon stockings to spend their pocket money on. They attended church services wearing their prettiest dresses for the choirboys. And, best of all for me, I could overhear their stories when they tried to outdo each other in their boasting during the lunch break.

I left the school at eighteen with good academic achievements. Again, I told my parents I wanted to be a nurse. This time, they gave me their consent, and the best advice they could possibly have done. 'Apply to one of the London teaching hospitals.'

From pamphlets available from career advisers, I chose one of the six, because it had a below-ground swimming pool for staff. I was accepted for training.

My childhood had been blessed by a family I took for granted.

And then I grew up.

*

I was to move into a large preliminary training school in Lancaster Gate not far from Marble Arch. The date, a Tuesday, loomed ahead as both an ending and a beginning. On the day, I gathered very few belongings to take with me because I was still preparing to return home every weekend. My mother offered to accompany me on the bus. It was February. We would have worn heavy winter coats and she probably added a hat.

As we left, my father kissed me goodbye and said, 'Bless you, my dear.' I had received many endearments from him over my childhood but never a 'bless you' before.

I was welcomed along with thirty-nine other new classmates. Bedrooms were allocated. Twin-share rooms. Alphabetical order. We were all girls. No male nurses were trained in these years.

Then my mother, with a few others, left us there, each preparing to share a room for three months with another eighteen-year-old we had never seen before.

This huge new home contained a school-like classroom, and a large practical room with scary things like hospital beds and sterilisers. There was a dining area and a lift between floors. In the corner of the big comfortable lounge room was a wooden table where later we would find laid out for us any mail that came.

We settled in. As a new set, with pride we put on the purple and white striped uniforms and white caps provided for us, and began our training.

Only an hour's journey from home, I was shocked by my debilitating homesickness. I couldn't sleep, and wasn't eating. Also, I had to be quietly taken out of lectures because I could not stop crying. I was counselled by our tutor sisters, older nurses who possibly, despite their kindness to me, sighed on the inside at my ineptitude. In answer to any question about it, I could only answer tearfully, 'I just miss them all at home.' Here I was at a place I had worked hard for with such anticipation, and out of a whole group of eighteen-year-olds I was the only one unable to deal with the new situation. It made no sense. During that time, I remember feeling a deep disappointment and also failure within myself. My homesickness did pass quickly as I made new friends, but I have never lost sight of the very real physiological incapacity and unhappiness it can cause.

During time off, identically dressed in our purple and white, we crossed the road to Hyde Park and, sitting in groups, practised bandaging each other. Elbows and heads proved most difficult, the latter causing much laughter both from us and from others walking in the park.

Back in the practical room, we rolled up our sleeves and added white aprons. We gave injections to oranges, and bed baths to each other. Any awkward embarrassment in this undertaking was soon dispelled as we either changed into a nightdress and climbed into the high hospital bed or we wore our uniform to perform our role. I see now that it was as much about learning how it feels to be dependent as about how to perform our tasks well. Also the beginning of a long appreciation of the benefit of wearing an outward sign of a profession.

This group was to remain my 'set' for the next years. All of us survived preliminary training, and the dreaded eighth week spent on the real wards of the hospital passed uneventfully as we were very gently integrated into the routines.

We worked on wards with twenty-four beds. When Matron was due to do a morning round, the wheels of every bed had to be perfectly aligned and pillowslips placed with the openings away from the entrance to the ward. And, very importantly, if we wanted to remain as probationers, we would never, ever, be seen to wear any make-up.

I was sent to a female ward where each patient went for their daily radium treatment for cancer. Most suffered relentless nausea across the twenty-four hours of each day. I felt valuable. I felt appreciated. I saw strong, resilient women coping with their misery, with never 'why me' or 'it's not fair'. I wondered for the first, but not the last, time in my life whether only the most exceptional people get cancer, or is it that cancer bring out the best in human beings?

One thing I knew without any doubt was that my decision to be a nurse was right for me.

At the end of that first three months of training came the big move to the main hospital nurses' home, duty rosters and hard work.

Living in London as the 1950s became the 60s. What a treat it was. However, as a group of eighteen-year-olds who thought we had moved out of home, we were in reality still very much provided for. Our meals were cooked for us, our uniforms laundered, and we had an evening curfew. I believe it was probably about ten-thirty, but it was possible to apply for a late pass. Theatres gave unsold tickets for productions for nurses which were, of course, always at the last moment. To see if any were available entailed a trip to Matron's office. They were not available to medical students so if there was a popular show in town, off-duty nurses were sought after to obtain some tickets to share. In exchange was the occasional pillion ride around the city on a motorbike.

If any of us expected to use the swimming pool beneath the hospital we were tested on our ability in the water. Grade A swimmers had to be able to swim a length of the pool and support another person safely in the water for ten minutes. Different times were allocated for male staff and for females. To go for a swim, there had to be at least three participants, two of whom had to be classed as A grade. I don't believe these rules were broken, for the very reason that they made sense. The pool was a long way below the busy hospital and appeared to be infrequently used.

Evenings off duty, however, were more often a gathering in someone's room with a couple of smuggled-in bottles of cider. We talked glibly about the popularity of Cy Laurie's Jazz Club in a basement in Great Windmill Street, but I don't think any of us were brave enough to find it and I don't believe Cy Laurie was there in person by the 1960s.

Music and movies we enjoyed. Elvis Presley wooed us with a 'Wooden Heart', we were 'Livin' Dolls' for Cliff Richard, and Helen Shapiro was often 'Walking Back To Happiness' on someone's transistor radio. Within a year, *Splendor in the Grass*, spelled the American way, Warren Beatty's first movie, was released in the States and became a craze world wide for young adults. Natalie Wood's voice over the closing scene, 'Nothing can bring back the hour of splendour in the grass, glory in the flower. We will grieve not, rather find strength in what remains behind', gave us what our great grandmothers would have called 'a fit of the vapours'.

And, of course, these were the years of trying to master the twist in our rooms ready for Chubby Checker's 'Let's Twist Again' on the dance floor should we ever be invited to a party. And there was an occasional dance or 'hop' at the medical school where, late at night, the students didn't simply leave without first announcing, 'I think I'll slough off now.'

We were all teenagers, and still doing a lot of growing up.

Fellow students, my friends, came from Wales, from Lancashire, and from Devon. I was fortunate to live close enough to go home on days off. The family had moved to an amazing three-storey house in Teddington, on the River Thames. Sometimes, if our days off coincided, friends came with me. A Green Line bus from Oxford Street tipped us out in the next road. Having someone to talk with kept me awake. Once later, exhausted, I slept to the terminus of the bus route and had to return on another bus.

My parents always made my friends welcome. My mother, fortunately for me, played the role of perfect mother, with beautiful home-cooked meals, followed by coffee in her beloved sunroom.

I might have found it hard to live down the suggestions my mother made when I came home alone. 'Come on, darling, you can never be too thin. We'll sit in the sunroom and have our coffee with a dexi, and a fag.'

She would have given us the cardigan off her shoulders if we were cold, and the food on her plate if we were hungry, but a dexi and a fag?

I, it appeared, at the age of eighteen, was an ally in the life of this suburban drug-pusher. Dexedrine tablets and cigarettes were obviously plentiful in this place of my growing up. I was gratified that to my friends my mother presented as a warm, caring and competent woman who loved to shop in South Kensington, and to whom a cup of coffee was just that.

Dad, as a consultant physician, lectured to nurses studying at his own hospital. This made him wonderfully valuable to me. After dinner at home on my days off during these training years, I would spread textbooks on the kitchen table. We returned, time after time at my request, to the functions of different organs of the human body. With elbows on the table, we gave this our full attention. I listened, I learned and I memorised words I understood. As I sought this help, I realised how fortunate I was. I also see now that, with his vast knowledge of physiology, how much pleasure it must have given my father to have a daughter who wanted to learn some of it. And Mother, washing dishes and putting away items not far away, listened and enjoyed every minute of it all.

Three months of every year were allocated to night duty. This involved packing our meagre possessions in one nurses' home, and walking with them, across the London streets, to find our new room in another one.

This huge residence specifically for night duty was a place of quiet days. Here cereal, toast and a cooked breakfast were served at seven o'clock in the evening, and dinner when we returned the next morning.

I think we believed we were in for an easy time watching over people who were asleep. And, being still in our late teens, sleeping all day and being awake all night sounded like fun.

We were wrong. We found the wards as busy at night as in the daytime and, worst of all, our own body clocks turned inside out and upside down. Daylight hours proved difficult for sleep, and many of us suffered nausea from the lack of it. We passed each other on meal breaks at different times in the night, the catchphrase becoming a muttered, 'Oh, for death and a long sleep.'

At that time, drugs to help us sleep as well as those to help us stay more alert were available to us, but only very occasionally did we resort to them.

Back on day shifts again, we sighed with relief, but every month brought new skills to be mastered and clinical facts to be learned.

*

Billy was fifteen years old and working in London in the 1960s. A sprawling grimy city full of life, full of people, all with their hopes and dreams. Billy was there with his own simple expectations, and I wasn't far away.

Billy served petrol at a city garage. He was proud of his first job, and he did it well. He had come from Ireland with his mother, and was helping by earning money for the two of them. However, on this day, Billy's pride was short-lived. Petrol spilled over his clothing, there was a stray match, and he was alight. In terror and panic, he did the only thing he could think of. He stumbled from the garage driveway, across the road and fell through the glass door of a café to reach his workmates. They were talking and laughing, but stopped abruptly as they stared in horror.

Billy was on fire. Billy was lacerated. Billy was beginning his death.

An ambulance siren sliced through the London streets.

I was a second-year nurse in the big old hospital to which he was taken. It was full of activity. Nights were as busy as days. Incredible things happened, and sick people got better. I was happy to be a part of it, and I loved the place intensely. I had been with patients when they died, and had witnessed my first birth in the middle of a winter night. After that, I climbed up onto the flat hospital roof in the early morning to reflect on the wonder of a new life. A first breath. A perfect infant. To go up onto the hospital roof was not allowed, but I bent the rules and watched the pallid sun rise over London.

A hospital must seem like a frightening maze of corridors and passageways to patients and visitors. It is a place full of busy people, but when you work in one it becomes familiar. On Billy's terrible morning, staff knew where they were expected to be, including me. I was to go to the sideward of the burns unit, where I was to 'special' a fifteen-year-old admitted from casualty.

I found Billy barely awake. 'Oh, Billy, what have you done? I'm here, though, kid. I'll take care of you.' Good grief, I was barely nineteen years old myself.

A pale woman in a thin woollen coat seated beside the bed gave me a weak smile. Billy's mother. She twisted an emerald-green scarf in her hands and her eyes begged for good news. I had none to offer. She scraped her chair out of my way as I approached the bed to make my efficient nursing assessment.

My care of Billy, along with other ward staff, continued for the next few days. At night, from my own small bedroom in the nurses' home, I could make out the window of the room where he lay. While the shaded light glowed, I knew that he lived on, and I returned each morning looking fresh and capable in my uniform.

Most of Billy's skin was scorched black. The house surgeon carefully slit each side of his charred fingers with a scalpel to release fluid and to give some comfort. Tears ran down all our faces as we shared the pain. We moved Billy as little as possible because he wasn't going to lie there long enough to get pressure areas. We wanted him to be comfortable. Regularly I gave the ordered doses of morphine and finally Billy lapsed into a coma.

His mother's vigil continued too. The gentle unassuming woman sat day and night beside the bed while care went on. She was quiet and never questioned any aspect of what we did for Billy. Sometimes, she laid her face on the counterpane and slept. At other times, she left the room for a short while, always being careful to place her scarf where her son would see it if he opened his eyes. She prayed constantly. I became used to the gentle murmurs she made to her god, and, as I recalled my physiology lectures, I knew it was a waste of time.

It took Billy four days and four nights to die. His kidneys finally failed and his organs shut down, which was, for medical staff, the expected outcome. The house surgeon and I gently laid out Billy's damaged body.

For his mother, it was the end of all hope. Her beautiful proud boy was dead. From my own privileged short life, I could only try to imagine her grief and her despair. Had her god failed her? After all those prayers? I was young, and I was knowledgeable, and yes, I was caring but I prided myself on my lack of need for divine assistance for this. I had learned facts I could accept. A gentle mother was told things she did not want to believe.

I remember now how I rationalised the whole concept with my friends, other teenage student nurses. The day that Billy died, I said, 'You know something? I don't think I believe in God any more. For four days, I have heard a woman pray to God to save her son, and I knew that it couldn't happen, so how does that work? Do we know things that God doesn't?'

Oh, dear heaven, the conceit, the absolute smugness of youth. How arrogant to assume that her entreaty was only for his recovery. How did I know that her prayers were not for his soul as it prepared to leave this earth? And what right had I to offer any judgement anyway?

I was, with competence and with care, doing my best for Billy, but looking back, I realise that in truth I never really saw his gentle mother, well…not in the way I would if I was part of that drama now. And I know why that was. I couldn't put myself in her place. I simply hadn't had the years of life. Now I could of course, but I guess I must accept the way I was at nineteen, as truly as I appreciate the way I am at this moment in time.

The way I am at this moment?

Life has come its full circle.

I too became that collective mother, and then grandmother, made vulnerable by love of a child. The memory of Billy and his mother makes me feel very humble. What an appalling heartbreak for any parent to experience. And what an outpouring of love and grief through prayer.

I also realise that my own little 'be safe' prayers for beloved children or grandchildren are, in comparison, little more than a simple talisman.

*

At the end of that second year, I went, with three other student nurses, to Austria for a two-week holiday. On the return journey, our flight was delayed, and we were unable to report for ward duty when expected.

The four of us were instructed to go to Matron's office. We filed in. I was first and we stood, demurely, in a row in front of her.

She said, 'I'll see you one at a time. Three leave and close the door.'

I heard, 'I'll see you some other time, please leave and close the door.'

When the three with good hearing trooped out, I went with them and closed the door carefully behind me.

After this perceived rudeness, I was banished to the Convalescent Hospital at Clacton-upon-Sea for six weeks.

Indignant, my mother threatened to 'go and see the matron about that'. I begged her, please, not to intervene on my behalf, and the six weeks I spent at Clacton turned out to be a treat. The huge old house was set in extensive grounds close to the seaside town. It was a perfect residence for patients, grateful to be recovering from illness or surgery, becoming stronger with each day, and preparing to return home. Nursing duties were light. We were more like housekeepers for their stay with us.

However, sometimes other problems had to be faced by our patients in addition to the slow recovery from illness. One man recuperating well from a heart attack was allowed by the resident doctor to walk to the nearby road and make his first bus trip into town. He returned distressed. He told us he had felt useless because he had had to stand by and watch, unable to assist, as a young woman struggled to get two small children and a pram onto the bus.

The return to general wards back in London brought further serious work, and study, with the prospect of final examinations. All those who successfully passed them after three years of training earned the silver badge of a state registered nurse. On the first day of our dreaded finals, as a group, fired with energy related to anxiety, we ran in our uniforms, along the London street outside the huge nurses' home and trooped under a ladder. We agreed that if we passed we would never, ever be superstitious again. We all passed.

The three years finished in February 1962, and I spent a further year as a staff nurse on a surgical ward. For that year, we were allowed to move out of the nurses' home, and with several friends I shared the two top floors of one of the huge old houses set in Fitzroy Square in London W1. We loved the address, but it was sparsely furnished and during the winter spent there, with only small electric fires, I felt colder than I had ever done before.

At the end of those twelve months, we all learned that we had passed our Hospital Finals, giving us our coveted Hospital badge. On that evening, each of us made a call to our family on the heavy black telephone in the hall of our flat. Most calls were more distant than mine and had to be booked through an operator, who became excited and happy for us all and offered his congratulations as well.

*

Some months later in the same year, I travelled to Australia with another nurse from my set. We had no interest in continuing with midwifery qualifications, and would like to have found work in France or Italy, but our language skills were completely inadequate. It was November 1963 and the Australian government was keen to attract trained people and young families from England. It cost ten British pounds and triggered the expression 'ten-pound Pom'. And, we rationalised, 'they do speak English in Australia'.

We travelled to Australia aboard the Sitmar Line *Castel Felice*. The ship, carrying 1,400 one-class passengers, was built in Glasgow in 1930, and later requisitioned by the British government as an armed infantry ship in World War Two. Between 1952 and 1970, on 101 voyages she carried over 100,000 immigrants to Australia and New Zealand, and I was one of them.

On our trip, with eight UK state registered nurses on board, the Australian federal health minister joined the ship for the Perth to Melbourne stretch and talked with each of us individually. He hoped to find out from us any ideas on how the government could attract more English-trained nurses to Australia.

December in Melbourne? Hot. Trams moving smoothly up and

down the streets, the tarmac outside Flinders Street Station soft underfoot, and businessmen wearing tailored shorts with long white socks.

Casual employment for London-trained nurses was not hard to find, and people with a flat to rent welcomed us without question. I don't think we realised how fortunate we were. As well trained as any in the world, we were just glad to be qualified, working and seeing Australia.

I wrote a letter every week to my parents, who were now retired in rural England. Phone calls had to be booked ahead and the time difference made it difficult. Letter writing was something I enjoyed, as I thought of them receiving my news. They too were diligent letter writers and airmail kept us fairly closely in touch.

Knowing that they were becoming older, I reflected that if something should happen to me, a kind friend could keep me alive for them during their lives through make-believe letters. A bizarre thought, but many years later in my life I adapted the idea within it as a one-act stage play.

I wrote *Affectionately Amanda* and set it in Perth in 1963. The play was performed in two independent theatres, directed by a friend, and won an award for new writing. Finding props for the set, which was a kitchen of the era, was a memory trip, but we found that Iced Vo Vo biscuits were still available.

Only three months later, the thought of living in Sydney enticed us into buying an old car and heading off up the 'one lane each way' Hume Highway,

*

A lot happened over the next years. I married an Englishman and we had our precious daughter and our equally precious son.

My small offspring, you are now all grown-up. However, this story full of memories, wonderful as I hope your stories are, is not yours.

Both my sisters with their husbands and children also moved from England to live in Sydney. Our beloved parents made two trips from England by ocean liner and finally packed up their home there to come and live in Sydney as well. Dad was happy to return but astonished that surfboard riders now stood up on their boards. Mum coped with the move but, although she said little about it, we were aware that she was incredibly sad and homesick to leave England.

Living in the Northern Beaches area of Sydney, my family once again was close to each other. Our parents got to know their grandchildren, and the young ones were in their turn blessed with love from them.

The families collected for a barbecue in the grandparents' garden most weekends. We three daughters who grew up in London were all now mothers. Three generations mingled and my sisters and I looked at each other knowing that roles were beginning, just a little, to reverse.

Mum was fulfilled preparing food for us all, and Dad was content to see everyone in their home and to have sons-in-law with whom to talk about life.

If anyone shivered on a cool evening Mum would say, 'Go and get a cardigan, darling, you know where they are.'

*

My third pregnancy ended at twenty weeks when, alone in our house, I delivered a tiny dead foetus in the bathroom. Complications led to two visits to the operating theatre. By the second time, I was terrified of the outcome. As I was wheeled into theatre, I made what I believed was the sign of the cross over my skinny chest. But was it up, down, left, right? I thought so, but I did a few other versions to improve my chances. I recall this now with the love and hope I see within it. Love? Yes, love or one of its many synonyms, for the thirty-two-year-old girl-woman that I was.

My parents and my sister were at the hospital and I know now what happened during that long session in theatre. My sister told me. Only because I asked her.

'They sent us home,' she said. '"We're going to lose her" was what someone from the theatre said. "Please go home and we'll phone you."

So we did, and we just sat there, and sat there. Mum with her head in her hands and Dad staring at the opposite wall. I don't know how long we sat like that and then shrill, shocking us all, the phone rang, And, of course, it was Dad who got up to answer it.'

I had come back to them.

My own knowledge of what made me come back has stayed with me.

While I was unconscious, in the peaceful blackness of forever, one image came. A picture of my small daughter and my smaller son, walking together along a path hewn by a lawnmower through foot-high grass. It was something I had witnessed the day before. I saw them now holding hands but maybe that was my own embellishment.

I woke finally, after major abdominal surgery, in severe pain. It appeared I was in intensive care and someone was telling me that my blood pressure was so low that sadly they could give me nothing for the pain.

'Could you give me a couple of panadol to take this away just a little bit?' I asked the nurse who came on duty for the night.

'Do you want to die?'

Defeated, I wondered why she had to be so unkind. No, I didn't want to die, so I didn't ask again.

With no pain relief, I lay awake through the night. I was aware that sometimes I groaned out loud. The skilled intensive-care nurse came to my bedside every fifteen minutes to take my pulse and record my blood pressure, but throughout her shift, never spoke any more words to me. She was an overweight girl. Maybe she was hoping for a boyfriend soon. Maybe she didn't feel like looking after a slim young woman who should have known better than to want three kids. It wasn't important. However, each time she stood beside me and touched my wrist, I realised that the pain diminished a little.

Finally, as light showed in the window frames, through tears I saw my mother stride towards my bed. I had to smile as well. She was doing her wonderful matron impression.

'They should have called me,' she announced loudly. 'I could have been here all night.'

I have never forgotten how my pain ebbed with her nearness and especially with her touch, as it had, to a lesser degree, with that of the overnight nurse. It is a phenomenon I have explained often and something I hope I have practised in my own life both personal and professional.

I begged to be moved out of intensive care. A place anywhere with nurses who smiled and spoke. Even a corridor they passed through would have done.

I was transferred to a bright cheerful ward where I was to remain for two weeks. There someone gave me access to Radio Something and I heard for the first time, and fell in love with, Neil Diamond's 'Song Sung Blue'. It was 1972.

What surprised me was that my own general practitioner came to see me late every afternoon as a visitor. I have learned that my complication was a very rare one, the kind that was documented in medical journals. Maybe he thought I was a little special. I saw him as another small part of the raft to which I clung.

On my journey home by car, the sky seemed huge and I wanted to cower from the vastness of a world that had forgotten me. I lived inside my own thoughts. I slept in a spare bedroom somewhere in the house, and listened to country and western music. I took a supportive friend up on her offer to help me with household chores. It was my choosing. I did it quietly and in my own way. And slowly I gained strength and began to feed my family, wash our clothes and clean the house again. My children still had their mother.

It appeared that the whole populace of our Sydney suburb knew what had happened. When I wandered through the shopping centre, people stopped and looked at me with reverence. They breathed sentiments. 'Oh, you poor thing.' 'What a dreadful experience.' But all of that meant little to me and, in my new existence, I wondered vaguely who these people were. It seemed they had their own Lazarus.

And as I write those words now, I revisit Sylvia Plath's complicated and dark poem 'Lady Lazarus' and return in my mind to my last days in London.

The fourth year as a staff nurse granted us the coveted Hospital badge. My four years were due to end on 10 February 1963.

That winter of our year at Fitzroy Square was the coldest in London for a hundred and fifty years. Water pipes froze solid, electricity failed, and train wheels froze on tracks. A chill pervaded the whole city. Residents became dispirited as temperatures continued to drop, and applications to immigrate to Australia reached peak numbers.

I learned some years later that the troubled poet Sylvia Plath had moved, with her two small children, into the upstairs part of a small flat in London that winter. It was there that her life was to end less than two months later. With only her beloved children for company, she was becoming more and more despondent.

On the night of 10 February, Sylvia put her children to bed in their attic bedroom. She left plates of bread and butter and two mugs of milk beside them for when they woke. No one knows the torment of that night but at about six o'clock the next morning she lay down to die. The gas from the oven not only filled her own flat, it also seeped through floorboards to render her downstairs neighbour unable to help. A new nanny, booked to arrive two hours later, went away, unsure of the correct address when there was no response to her knocks on the door. A note in the flat asked for Sylvia's doctor to be called but it was too late.

On the very same day that, at twenty-two, I completed my training, she was planning, at the age of thirty-one, to die.

My first return to work after being so ill was a couple of evening shifts a week at a local nursing home. There, I found myself caring for the mother of the big-hearted, skilled obstetric consultant who saved my life in the operating theatre. To live, I know now, more than another forty years of life.

He lay across his mother's bed on many evenings, sharing tumblers of whisky and packets of cigarettes. I smiled on the inside. He contravened no rules, except perhaps, just a little, those of common sense. I thought maybe one day the tableau might be me with my son, who might care as much in his own way.

I wonder too now whether it was simply a coincidence that I was there or was it perhaps a lovely preordained way to enable me to give a little back.

*

My beloved mother is there when I nearly die, and nine years later our roles are to reverse. In 1981, she dies in the home in Sydney she shares with Dad.

I am forty-one years old when this happens, and I am closely involved. It is an experience that is to remain close to my heart for the rest of my life. Always there beneath the surface of my conscientious professional world.

Reminiscences overlap. Pieces of the jigsaws of life's memories are put in place at different times. Four years after the death of Mother, Dad has become accepting of living alone when my life, living near to him, begins a big change.

My husband is offered a transfer to Perth for better work opportunities. His company pays for me to spend a week there to share the decision to move. It is 1985 and Perth presents almost like a big safe country town. I am captivated by the thought that our young ones, now sixteen and eighteen years old, can continue their lives in this city.

We buy a house south of the Swan River, with a granddad flat attached, and promise my dad that it is his whenever he would like, or have a need, to come to Perth.

Everything we own is transported across the Nullarbor Plain on a semi-trailer to Western Australia, and we settle into new lives.

We acquire a young bull terrier, a stray nobody wants, and we name her Jemma. We are not to know in those early years that she is to become a loyal friend, companion and comfort to four generations.

Dad does come to live with us a little later in all of our lives. I am rewarded by his willingness to do so but after three years he dies in a nearby nursing home. And I am with him.

His death in 1990 is the same year that a divorce means that I have to return to full-time work.

I am fifty years old.

*

I study for a Palliative Care certificate through a Perth university in preparation for working in that area of nursing.

Our lectures are given and our practical work done at the Perth Cottage Hospice. I appreciate studying again, and I grow to feel affection for the other registered nurses learning with me. We receive lectures from doctors who know all there is to know about palliative care, and we are allowed to talk with patients at this final stage in their lives.

Elisabeth Kubler-Ross, born in 1926 in Switzerland, was the psychiatrist who documented the five stages of the grief of knowing one is going to die. Denial. Maybe there's been a mistake. Anger. Why me? It's not fair. Bargaining. If I'm allowed to get better, I promise to change my lifestyle. Depression. Why bother with anything? And, finally Acceptance. She studied medicine in America, married a fellow medical student, and died in Arizona in 2004.

We also looked at the work of the English Anglican nurse, medical social worker and physician, Cicely Saunders, born in 1918, and founder of the modern hospice movement. She was educated at Roedean School, and studied to be a nurse at St Thomas's Hospital in London during the war years. She returned there later to become a doctor.

Cicely Saunders began fundraising for St Christopher's Hospice in London the year I left for Australia. It was opened four years later, but it was not for another twenty years that the Royal College of Physicians recognised palliative care as a medical specialty.

Cicely Saunders was awarded Dame of the British Empire in 1979.

She was cared for at the end of her life in her beloved St Christopher's Hospice, where she died in 2005. She was much loved by the staff there, and nearly two thousand people attended a service of thanksgiving for her life at Westminster Abbey.

Most people understand that palliative care means pain will be covered and discomfort relieved. Good palliative care covers many other aspects at the end of a life. Spiritual, cultural and emotional needs are also addressed. Visiting is unrestricted, and loved pets are often made welcome.

As a place of care, the hospice was very specific. The outcome for each patient there was already defined but I remember the warmth in the environment. The love within the hospice was palpable. It reminds me now of words Pope Benedict used on the second anniversary of the death of Pope John Paul II. 'His love for Christ was without reserve or limit. The perfume of his love filled our house, the church.' A beautiful use of synaesthesia as a literary term, where one sense is used to describe another.

I do not presume to elevate medical and other staff members to the status of the beloved Pope John Paul, but simply as a few humble human beings with love of a similar kind. If not for God, for the work they carried out every day.

At this time, the late 1980s, the Perth Cottage Hospice was preparing to set aside wards for patients with acquired immunodeficiency syndrome, AIDS. My name was on the list for staff on the wards, but the shocking expected outbreak did not occur. And those who did become HIV-positive were mostly nursed by family and friends, and died at home.

*

I decided to take my knowledge of palliative care into the nursing home sector. I was initiated in reiki healing, and also achieved a Gerontology Certificate from a large public hospital.

I began full-time work.

I don't believe anyone would choose to go into long-term aged care.

Most people in the middle years of life, who know they are never going to be young again, cannot envisage the end of their life in a care facility. Nearly all would express the wish to die peacefully in their own bed.

Truth is that death is available all the time, everywhere. And, while bridges, motorways, high-rise buildings, oceans and lakes offer a swift ending, most people choose to go on living. And life is a treasured option, but not if it becomes weighed down with pain, loss of independence or lack of dignity.

It amounts to a juggling act, because once you are in care, you have lost your chance. Nursing homes exist to keep people alive. You will be watched over, and maintained at room temperature. Your sleeping hours will be monitored, and you will be turned over every so often by a couple of people who may be chatting to each other about the party they went to the evening before. You will not be scrutinised for a use-by date.

I recall going to check on one of my residents late one evening, and she said, 'Oh, I thought it was the ten o'clock turn over.' Imagine having to wait while seconds tick by, to be assisted to move in your own bed. And I imagine now that same small person. Curled waiting for sleep. What were her thoughts? Her memories? Were there unspoken worries or concerns?

You will also have to wait for a chance to get off the planet when no one is looking. By then, you will be so fed-up with your existence that you will have given up caring, and you will sigh deeply each morning as you are hoisted out of bed for the day.

Aged care facilities are overflowing with people who have led fulfilled and happy lives, now unable to hold a simple conversation or feed themselves. Look into the eyes of a stroke victim with full mental capacity but unable to speak or swallow. Liquid food can be poured through a 'peg' in their abdomen while their eyes plead for help. In the case of pneumonia, antibiotics can be added. Achievement? Kept alive as long as humanly possible? A strange concept in this context.

There is, however, a wonderful empathy underpinning the final care in some nursing homes, which breaks no law. It is the understanding of true compassion, of genuine kindness. To support an individual, or distressed family members on their behalf as decision maker, that enough is enough. To be non-aggressive, and, despite the fact that doctors are duty-bound to prescribe them, to accept that pneumonia has existed much longer than antibiotics.

I believe that many sons or daughters feel that they may be judged, and I counselled many times that that would not be the case. They would receive support, not censure. And it is the nurses who see those pleading eyes hour after hour, day after week after month, so if those same nurses should, as a team, lose those antibiotics down the sink? Well, that couldn't happen. Could it?

It did happen. With understanding and unspoken words. Doctors knew. Relatives wept with relief at the possibility to bring forward the inevitable,

And, working only occasionally within these parameters, I found a message. Early communication within families. For all of us, to talk with our loved ones about what we would choose at the end of life has to be a good thing. We need to address the subject although it may be a challenge and perhaps harrowing.

On weekend shifts, I often found myself responsible for the whole ninety-eight-bed nursing home with a team of superb carers, a junior registered nurse and another provided by an agency. There was no receptionist, no management, and doctors were hard to contact if needed. If the kitchen staff ran out of milk, they came to ask me what they should do.

As I drove through the deserted streets, I said small prayers to any higher being listening at six forty-five in the morning. God of all nurses be with me in my decisions today.

Please.

I also estimated that at the bare minimum of seventy years per resident under this roof, between them they had experienced over six and a half thousand years of life.

The child who is born on the Sabbath day, as the nineteenth century nursery rhyme states, is a special child. Maybe the Sabbath is also a special day upon which to die, for it seemed to happen often.

One of two elderly sisters in room nine died early one Sunday morning. Night staff had talked with family, done all the paperwork and contacted the funeral director. I sat with Jessie later in the morning as behind a curtain her sister's body was prepared to be taken away. We talked quietly amid the rustle of plastic sheeting. Although Jessie seemed to cope with it all, tears ran down my face as I thought of my own sisters. Later, I wrote in my journal, 'What a job. Why on earth did I ever think I wanted to become a nurse?'

Now, I wonder whether Jessie and her sister had talked long into nights together as they faced the next journey. Maybe Jessie would have preferred to be going too.

Occasionally, there was some light relief. One morning, I was informed by one of my residents, 'We knew you were here, we heard you singing.' It was something one could do with the lesser formality of weekends and if all was going well. They became used to 'Busted flat in Baton Rouge, waiting for a train', at seven o'clock on many mornings. Not only did I turn up for the day but also Bobby McGee.

And my ridiculous question. 'What do you get from Surprise Peas?'

'Wet legs of course.'

A wonderful endless joke that could be shared and enjoyed over and over again.

I instigated T-shirt Sundays. Just for that one day, I encouraged all the carers on my wing to wear an interesting or attractive T-shirt instead of their uniform shirt. 'Come in one that shows the residents something of your world.' Some were loath to break rules but occasionally we all arrived in a top or shirt a little bit more fun. 'Nobody's Perfick' was there among the sports logos and the pop stars, and conversation with residents was often prompted. I chose a simple flowered blouse.

When I was young, I had romantic ideas about the white caps and navy capes worn by nurses. Throughout our training in London, uniforms had been supplied for us, and laundered, by the hospital. We saw them as the clothes we wore for work, and had more fun shopping for off-duty outfits in the stores of London. Hats and gloves were desirable accessories, and considered the epitome of fashion. Wide-brimmed hats in particular were likely to attract whistles from a building site.

I believe now that a uniform can benefit both those doing the caring, and a patient. For a nurse, it gives identification, but it can also act as a shield. Something that can come between the wearer and confronting or unpleasant things that have to be dealt with that fall outside everyday life experiences.

Back in my training hospital days, patients occasionally donated their eyes after death for corneal grafting. I must have been in my third year when I was asked to hold a torch for the house surgeon from the eye ward as he removed the eyes of a deceased man. It was performed in a sideward with curtains drawn out of respect. I suppose I could have closed my own eyes and hoped for the best but I found myself asking permission to leave the room before I fainted.

Not a pleasant experience. However, I was asked to perform the same task a couple of months later. This time, the young white-coated house surgeon was new to the eye ward and it was his first time. He seemed more frightened of the experience than I. On this occasion, I found myself not only holding the torch steadily for the whole procedure but also talking quietly to the young doctor and telling him how well he was doing. Somehow, we both got through the process without passing out.

But imagine too the value of a uniform that perches on the bed of an unwell person and enquires about intimate functions of that body. I liked the title 'sister' for the same reason. Once, however, on answering the telephone at work with the words 'Good morning, Sister speaking,' I was confronted by my daughter's exclamation, 'Heavens above, Mother, you've become a nun.'

On one early Monday shift, the receptionist demanded to know whether anyone had used her typewriter over the weekend because it was making a funny noise. When she looked more closely at it, she discovered a lower set of dentures in it. I found this wonderfully amusing but she couldn't even smile. They were returned to a resident with Alzheimer's disease who seemed surprised to see them again.

*

A difficult thing happened on a weekend. One Sunday, when it came to lunchtime, I chose to feed my sickest patient myself. He was ninety years old, had bronchopneumonia, and had almost stopped eating.

I removed the crusts from two slices of bread, buttered them well, sprinkled sugar on top, and cut them into small squares. The easiest lunch ever created. One at a time, I put them into his mouth and he appeared to relish them, chomping happily with his ninety-year-old teeth.

And then he bit through two of my fingers.

I was angry. With myself. How could I be so careless? I also knew that as well as the pain of it, a human bite can lead to serious infection so I rang the emergency department at the local large public hospital. A nurse on duty told me I would need a tetanus booster and broad-spectrum antibiotics.

I was teased a lot by my colleagues about lockjaw. Fortunately for me, a doctor called in unexpectedly, told them not to be so silly, and provided me with the scripts I needed.

My elderly patient died before I finished the antibiotics.

It got worse.

*

Victor had been a difficult resident to manage in our nursing home. A big man and physically strong, he was severely demented and was often aggressive with staff. His frequently used tactic was to grab someone's hand and, using all his strength, bend the thumb back on itself. I live with residual arthritis in my left wrist from this injury.

One of my tasks was to ensure that residents in my care received their daily medication. Most were prescribed several tablets twice or more often each day. One morning, Victor spat his pills crushed in jam back in my face. I stepped back and wiped my face with the back of my hand. I wanted to smack him like a badly behaved toddler. No, worse. Silently, I wished him dead. Defeated, I went to clean up, knowing I would have to return later.

Victor also frequently attempted to abscond from the premises. On one occasion, we searched the buildings and grounds for him. After doing that, I was supposed to notify the police. However, I knew which way he had headed before, so why waste police time. I went to look for him in my old 144 Volvo, and there was Victor on the other side of the busy road. I did a U-turn, stopped the car beside him, got out, opened the rear door and ordered, 'Get in.'

After glaring at me for moments, he did so. I was thankful, as I had no plan to deal with defiance and would not have chosen to ask passers-by for help. On reflection, it would have been better to request police assistance to find him and bring him back.

On return, it was my duty to telephone Victor's wife and inform her that he had absconded yet again. Her response was brief. Her response was loud. 'Tie him to a chair.'

To restrain a patient in that way was not allowed in the book of rules, but I might, on that occasion, have felt obliged to honour her request.

Victor's condition deteriorated slowly over several weeks. Transfer to a psychiatric facility was mooted, but his wife liked him being in our care, so we struggled on. He was treated for pneumonia and became more frail.

On one of my Sunday afternoons, he was fed a little lunch, but collapsed suddenly. I was able to contact his wife who visited before he died, and nominated a funeral director, but a doctor did not attend till later. He was from one of the medical deputising services, and provided only a Life Extinct Certificate.

Some of this I wrote in a report on our care of Victor for the state coroner because of what transpired the following day.

From my own journal the following day:

Work 6.45 Commented to the Clinical Nurse Specialist that the only real concern with Victor's sudden death yesterday was that his doctor hadn't seen him for twelve days. She said, 'That shouldn't be a problem,' but shit, about 11 a.m. I was called to the Director of Nursing's office. She had had the police on the phone. Since there was no cause of death certificate, it was to be a coroner's case. I had, without any right, released the body to the undertaker. I was to write a report for the coroner, photocopy all the doctor's notes, find the coronial enquiry office in Subiaco by 1.30 p.m. and go from there to the city morgue and identify the body. Holy shit.

I was released from my normal nursing duties for the day to do this.

I rang home to see what my son was doing. 'Uni,' he said, so I thought I'd just take a taxi. I was pretty uptight.

However, my daughter rang back. 'I'm on a day off, and I'm bored stiff. I'll take you and then we'll have a drink somewhere.' What a wonderful girl.

I asked her to raid my bathroom and bring me more antiperspirant, more deodorant. Anything she could see there.

We found the Coronial Enquiry Office that afternoon, its doorway onto a busy city street, and went in. A police officer greeted us. He was expecting me and took my handwritten 'to whom it may concern' report. He was to drive me to the city morgue. Such a courteous, pleasant, well presented officer that my daughter in her twenties asked if she could come too.

'No,' he said, 'just your mother.'

He drove me to the nearby big city hospital.

My memory of entering the viewing room is of a couch, chairs, a table with a carafe of water, glasses, and a box of tissues. A curtain covered one wall. I wondered what might have happened in this horrible, disinfectant-smelling little room. Had people sobbed? Fallen to their knees in prayer? Collapsed completely? And what did this police officer I was with do if so? Vaguely, I thought that he must have an emergency call button somewhere.

He closed the door, and we stood there.

'Are you ready?' he asked.

And when I nodded, the curtain was drawn back.

It was a man. It could have been any elderly man. The body was covered, the face in profile, and the neck extended because he lay flat on a slab. We never covered a face either. He, or she, I would say, will just look as though asleep. And always I stroked the forehead to indicate that it was all right to touch.

I felt quite remote. This was not as I had last seen Victor, dead indeed, but tucked up in bed with blankets and a pillow. I simply said, 'Yes, that's him,' and I remember hoping sincerely that it was.

Thinking back over the last moments on the short walk back to the police car, I made the comment to the officer that I imagined I must be an easy one for him.

'Yes,' he said. He was quiet for a moment, and then he added, 'Yesterday, I escorted a long-haul truck driver to identify his sixteen-year-old son.'

God, I thought. Who'd be a cop? I also hoped that wearing a uniform that he could take off at the end of a harrowing day might help to put things into perspective.

And then it was over. My daughter took me to the nearest tavern, and bought me two gin and tonics in fairly rapid succession.

'Do you want to eat here?' she asked.

'Oh yes.' And from the menu I chose lambs fry and bacon, which somehow sounded right for that moment in time. Strange, because I thought of myself as a vegetarian, but it appeared that there must really be something about the perception of food being a comfort.

When I got home later, the house was quiet. I lay on my bed in my uniform and increasingly I needed to talk to someone. I rang a friend, a theatre nurse in a big private hospital.

She said she'd had a shithouse day and was just going to have her tea, so I said, 'Okay, have your meal, call me back and I'll trade you shithouse days.

That night, I found it difficult to sleep. Making tea at three o'clock in the morning, I wondered if I had done enough. Would there be any repercussions?

There was never any response to my report to the coroner's office, but a few days later an announcement for Victor's cremation was published in *The West Australian*. The coroner must have been satisfied with my report, without need for an autopsy. Later, I learned that many sudden deaths that reach the coroner's office are dealt with at desktop level so I guess this was one of those.

*

Another Sunday, and I find another gentleman, close to ninety, has been fed his tea and died quietly in his bed. Even while I'm going for a stethoscope, my mind is racing ahead. Ring the family. Of course. Get a locum doctor to ascertain life extinct. Get a priest? Oh God. No, not God, just a priest. And still I doubt my own conclusion that someone is dead beyond any doubt. Nurses do not make that assertion even if it is obvious. Trained to state only that breathing has ceased, I once used those words on the phone to a resident's general practitioner. After a pause, he asked, 'And what are you going to do about it, Sister?'

But, today, I look at the telephone for moments knowing that I have to pick it up. No one is going to do it for me. And I do call the family, aware that the words I am choosing to say may be remembered for a long time.

Back at work the next day, there were more problems. On many, many occasions, a deceased resident was taken to an undertaker's premises with the presumption that a cause of death certificate would follow. However, the doctor of the man who had died suddenly was out of the country, so the Coronial Enquiry Office was again involved.

The resident's daughter and her husband visited to collect belongings, and told me there appeared to be no lack of responsibility, but they had been asked to identify his body at the city morgue. Not surprisingly, the thought of it distressed both of them.

'No, I'll go,' I told them and this time I drove my own car there and completing the task in not much more time than my evening meal break.

I still have the little terracotta angel and the thank you letter from his daughter.

*

It wasn't all unhappiness. We had fun as well.

On an evening shift, a friend phoned to ask if I would like her to drop in with half a bottle of champagne that she and a guest hadn't finished. I met her in the front car park with a wheelchair. We stood the recorked bottle in the chair and draped a draw sheet around its neck.

'Meet Pin Head', we told the residents as we wheeled him respectfully through the front door. Suddenly with a loud bang, Pin Head's head flew off and hit the ceiling.

I was occasionally badly behaved too.

One evening, I carried back to the physio room a by-then-cold heat pack, wrapped in a white towel. As I passed residents sitting in the foyer, I made believe I was holding a tiny baby, indicating rocking it gently and gazing fondly down at it. Then I pretended to trip and allowed the poor little heat pack to fly out of my arms onto the floor.

Shrieks of concern then laughter from the assembled grandmothers and grandfathers was good for the soul.

Well, I hope it was. I do know that not one of them had a cardiac arrest.

During one week, we worked with repairs being carried out in the roof space. Often, strange noises came from above us. Looking at the ceiling from time to time, we joked that if someone was to fall through, with ninety-eight beds below they would be unlucky not to land on one. And it happened. A young man crashed through onto the end of the bed of an elderly lady.

Hearing the noise, I was there very quickly. The feisty nonagenarian was incensed at the intrusion into her quiet morning. She glared at him, her little fists going up and down, beating the air, ready to take him on.

'Sorry,' muttered the young man. 'Really sorry about that,' and climbed off the bed.

The resident, the much-loved grandmother of one of our state footballers, was good enough to laugh, just a little bit, about it later. I hope that the young roofing carpenter told the little story to his mates later too.

I wondered if drivers on the busy road outside, passing on their way to work, could have any idea what went on within our walls. Young male carers, still almost boys, taking other young men's grandmothers for a warm shower, while yet another was falling through the ceiling.

To find young people who enjoyed their employment or work experience with the elderly was heartwarming.

One morning, a young physiotherapy student walked slowly past me at the front desk with one of our residents. He addressed the memory loss of dementia with kindness in his words to me, 'Neither this gentleman nor I can remember his name.'

*

Letting go when the moment is right? Hanging on to life? I have seen both.

Occasionally, it appears that there is a simple wish to die when alone. To take advantage of a short space of time when no one is present. Too often not to have some credence, I have talked with distressed loving people who say, 'But we were only away for about fifteen minutes.'

Often, it is a comfort to know that this has happened to others. Maybe in essence it can be seen as a desire to save them the anguish of being present. And can it be possible to enable death by unspoken permission?

I have also, very occasionally, if I felt it would be a comfort in the grief, told them that I was there. A white lie if there is such a thing, but still not truth.

Towards the end of yet another weekend shift, another grandfather was close to his moment of death, but his beloved family was still over an hour away on their long drive to be with him. I knew that he could hang on. Pulling a chair beside his bed, I placed the phone between us and sat writing my report on what had happened over the shift. Each time the telephone rang, I relayed their message. 'Tell him we've just reached…' 'And now we're passing through…' I touched his hand every time I spoke, and then replaced the phone once again between us on the bed cover. His irregular shallow breaths continued as together we waited.

On their arrival, it seemed as though his family bounded in, and exuberant small children climbed onto the bed. And why not? I think I remember a small dog too, but I do believe that is probably in my imagination.

Life is a series of snapshots and as such is always in past tense. Smile for the camera, we say, and collect, in whatever form, photographs of people doing so. How I would love a snapshot of that moment. A grandfather with his children and their children needing to hug him goodbye.

He died before I went off duty that evening, but I left in wonder once again at the strength and resilience of the human soul when life is failing.

*

On another morning, I arrive for work at six forty-five a.m. and take over from my colleague who has now finished her night shift. As we complete our handover, the phone rings. We're informed that a television in one of the units at the rear of the nursing home has been blaring all night, and is still disturbing those who live nearby.

'I'll go,' says my colleague, taking a master key.

I begin my first medication round, the 'take before breakfast' pills of the day. I hear the phone ring again and a carer comes to tell me I'm needed urgently over at the units. I have to leave my patients and I run, thinking, 'Oh God, what's happened?'

My colleague meets me at the door of the small unit, and together we enter the lounge room. Heavy brown curtains cover the windows, and there is a stale smell of cooking. The television that has been annoyingly loud is now silent. Solid wooden furniture stands on worn carpet, and between two armchairs, a newspaper is open on a coffee table. The occupant of the room lies sprawled on the floor.

And time stands still.

We both know that this man has been dead for many hours. As nurses, we have no authority to certify the fact. Call an ambulance, or call a doctor? In whispers, we discuss our options. Only briefly. We have to call paramedics or the family may ask why we didn't do so. This death has happened suddenly and was not expected.

I dial triple zero from the unit, and talk with some understanding person about what has happened.

'Yes,' she says, 'I'll send an ambulance.'

The only thing I ask is please, can they come quietly, without lights or siren. This, I explain, is a retirement village. 'Let's not scare them to death,' and it is not said as any sort of joke.

More difficult is the call to the man's family, who live north of the river. I'm aware that it comes as a complete shock, but his daughter says she will be here as soon as she possibly can.

Together, my colleague and I wait at the unit till the ambulance arrives very soon afterwards. There is confirmation that nothing can be done except to make the gentleman look more comfortable for the family. He is a big man. He has slid down awkwardly against a chest of drawers, and we've not moved him. The two paramedics gently settle him on the floor. We find a pillow and a rug as they leave.

I'm aware of a feeling of intrusion in this private space. The home of a man who, the evening before, had turned on his television and drawn the curtains across the windows. For the last time.

'I'll stay.'

The quiet words bring me back to the present.

'I'll wait with him till his family gets here.'

This from a nurse who has already been on duty for ten hours, and has a husband and school-age children waiting for her to share breakfast.

I do, though, with extreme gratitude, return to the duties of my own shift. A day job that's never the same from one hour to the next.

It appears that paramedics can certify that death has occurred. I have learned that they are able to do a lot of things that nurses can not, and also many that doctors can.

*

Later in life, I wrote a short story based on things that happened over this time in my life. 'Angela's Bus Trip' was indeed a fun thing to talk about with my beloved residents on days when for them not a lot happened. I explained to the director of nursing that it was a fantasy in case she thought I was contemplating dispatching inmates to heaven, but she only smiled.

I attempted to tell my story through the eyes of one of the many sons I met, cared about and never saw again. I respected them for their commitment at the end, and fell just a little in love with each and every one.

I called myself Anna.

I Liked Anna

Anna was what every man needs when his frail and bewildered mother is admitted to a nursing home.

I liked the way she stroked Mother's arm as she said, 'I hope I can care for her as I would like my mother to be cared for.' If these were Anna's first words, when any resident was admitted I didn't care. I was new to this. I found it comforting.

Over the next weeks, Anna was often at the nursing home when I visited. To me, most of what went on seemed a vaguely organised shambles, but it met the needs of the oldies and released me from mother minding. God knows I needed that. and Anna seemed to love it all. She was welcome to it, and I continued to like both her and her cheerful smile.

Once settled into the nursing home, Mother became withdrawn, and hardly ate anything. Whenever I visited, she mumbled that she didn't want to live any more.

'Of course you do.' Frustrated, I became impatient.

She stopped talking about her feelings.

One morning when I visited, breakfast was in progress in the big dining room.

Anna noticed a gentleman spooning porridge into his dressing gown sleeve. 'No, Giovanni, please, don't do that.'

He let forth a torrent of Italian.

'*Per favore*, Giovanni, English?'

'Piss off.' He did speak English.

Anna sighed, and taking the spoon began patiently to feed the man his breakfast. Seeing me, she smiled and, despite the mess of porridge dribble, I was captivated.

Many of the nursing home residents talked about Anna's bus trip. When Mother's room-mate told Anna she would like to be dead, she was given her medication with the words 'Sweetie, if there was a bus going straight to heaven, I'd make sure you were the first person on it.' Most of the oldies seemed happy to contemplate the idea; one elderly man even offered to drive the bus. 'Anna's bus trip'? It offered hope, and their longed-for escape to the celestial home.

Months passed. Mother became weaker, was often confused, and no longer smiled when I visited. I wondered sadly how it was all going to end.

Then, early one morning, Anna phoned to tell me Mother had developed pneumonia and was refusing to swallow antibiotics. Respecting her wishes, we agreed that treatment should be passive.

Mother's condition deteriorated and I took days off work to sit beside her bed. Tentatively, briefly, at times I held her hand. I also walked up and down the corridors or picked at takeaway food. I brought in whisky for the nights, borrowed blankets and dozed fitfully next to the bed.

On her shifts, Anna came in with morphine and I went for coffee. While a team of nurses went in to attend to Mother, I could go for a shower.

However, eventually the long vigil was over. Mother was safely on the bus.

Exhausted, I took Anna's hand. 'I know it may sound strange, but that was a truly incredible experience. Thank you.' She smiled at me for the last time, and I walked out into the evening.

I never saw Anna again.

*

That was how Angela's bus trip began. Transport straight to heaven?

This concept was to trigger another memory for me. There was something those hopeful of being dispatched on the bus didn't know. They could not know about four days that had once had such an impact upon my life.

Only I knew, and I return to what had happened when my own mother died.

My mother, at seventy-six, almost nine years after I had almost died, was in the last stages of cancer first discovered in her colon. She had undergone extensive surgery, but now had a spread to her liver. She and Dad lived a few streets away from me, and he told us, each of his daughters, individually. I remember his arm around my shoulders as he said, 'I'm so sad, my dear, but there's nothing more that can be done to help her.' And with those words, the final grieving began, as did my mother's increasing pain.

My parents had, for as long as I was old enough to understand, believed strongly in voluntary euthanasia. Having cared for Dad's mother after a severe stroke for several years in our home, my own mother treasured the thought of a dignified end to her own life.

She had kept a poem by Charles Blackshield, the first verse of which states,

> There should be dignity in death,
> Not soiled sheets and rancid breath;
> Why should we have to linger on
> When continence and sense are gone?
> I fear not death, and do not wish to be
> Diminished by senility.
> I claim the right to choose to die
> While sense remains, and I am I.

'…and I am I'. What wonderful words. As a family, we understood her wishes and we also knew she had the tablets she needed to end her life. On one evening in late October 1981 after one of my usual visits, I remember having a feeling that she was going to take them that night.

Early next morning, the phone rang in my kitchen. It was Dad, and in his usual thoughtful way he said, 'When you've got the kids off to school, my dear, can you pop in?'

I left in my car within minutes. I pulled into the driveway of my parents' modest brick and tile house a few streets away, where the barbecues in the back garden had brought the family together most weekends. Their bedroom window faced the street. The curtains were closed. I thought, 'My mother is dead', and with relief my thinking shifted into, 'It's nearly over.'

My father met me.

'She took her pills?' I asked.

He answered my question with the same four words, and then he added, 'but she's still here.'

I thought he meant that her body was still in the bed next to his.
No.

'She's still breathing,' he said.

Breathing? I went to see her. 'Jesus, Dad, what the hell happens now?' My blasphemies were, I know, forgiven from above.

My mother had settled into her bed to watch her favourite television program, *A Country Practice*. Not, however, with a few biscuits and a glass of sherry, but with a vial of barbiturates, and a whole bottle of brandy.

But the pills she had taken were not sufficient.

Mother, I want to look into your mind now, and realise how many years too late I am. What were your thoughts as you lay waiting for sleep? Sleep from which you would not expect to wake. Did you cry quietly? I lean against the windowpane of the years that separate us. I see wasted opportunities, frittered time, and know that soon, I too shall be in that transparent space. Wondering what happens next.

Over the next few days, you began to wake up.

Vaguely, I thought maybe we have stumbled on the cure for cancer. Take almost enough but not quite sufficient pills to cause death. It was of course not to be.

You seemed aware of your surroundings but I believe your vision was impaired. My sisters visited and you began to speak a few words. One of my sisters helped me to wash you, and move you gently and frequently. After a time, as you became increasingly restless, I drove across local suburbs trying to purchase a catheter in order to keep you comfortable. Finally, in desperation, I went to the emergency department of the nearby hospital, where a caring nurse was glad to be able to give me what I needed.

'I can do this,' I told my sister, 'but I really do need you to help me.'

Together, we catheterised our mother. It was a procedure I understood well, but strange and intimate in the privacy of our parents' bedroom. However, we achieved our aim and restlessness ceased.

It was a time in limbo. My mother's doctor visited and asked no questions when it was obvious that something had happened. He was an older man, a true family doctor, with years of experience. He was a precious human being with skill and knowledge. I also believe he possessed the ability to turn a blind eye.

With the slow awaking, it was obvious that my mother's severe pain began to return. She groaned as tears squeezed from her eyes. What to do? Caught up in this terrible time, I knew it was my decision.

I asked the same doctor for ampoules of morphine, and an antiemetic by injection to stop her from feeling sick.

*

My mother was fed tablets to cause her death. No, be truthful. I fed them to her. I crushed, and crushed, and crushed those damn pink pills. With the pestle, in the mortar she had probably used for black peppercorns and herbs over the years before. More tablets than needed to make sure. I mixed them with jam and I cannot imagine what they tasted like.

She opened her mouth each time for the spoon, and must have known what I was doing as she swallowed those disgusting pills. I suppose I talked to her as I did it but not too sentimentally, more matter of fact. I was doing my job with care and I can say to the rest of the world, 'But you weren't there, were you.'

And how do you measure love.

Then I told Dad that I'd come back later, and I drove home to prepare a meal for my family as though it was just another ordinary late afternoon.

I did return. My parents' house was quiet. My mother, in her bed, was taking irregular shallow breaths. My father and I went to the kitchen where, for some reason, we found ourselves whispering. We had thirty-milligram ampoules of morphine and we both knew at this stage what just one would do.

I believed my father could do this for her but he said, 'My dear, I'd rather you gave it.' And in that moment, I felt anger. Doctor's orders? He was a long-retired medic. I was a practising registered nurse. He could have taken that last bit from me. Hadn't I already done enough?

Maybe I also learned in that moment that love and hate are partners within our lives, and that at times love knows a glimpse of hatred, while hate can understand fleeting affection. I gave my beloved mother morphine that had been ordered for her. It was late evening now. I went home. Again.

Within an hour, I received the phone call to tell me that that it was finally over. By now, I was beyond a response in words. I hung up the phone, and sat with my head in my hands and sobbed, till I realised my two children, thirteen and fifteen, were standing helpless in my grief.

Oh God. I took a deep breath and got out the words. 'I'm okay. Granny has died, but really, sweeties, everything will be all right.'

Next morning, I visited Dad, said a quiet final goodbye to my beautiful mother, and told him, 'When her GP comes, be a bit vague. Say your daughter was looking after it all.' And I ran away.

Looking back at that time as the woman I am now, I wonder why I didn't stay.

My future as a nurse hung, clichéd, upon a doctor signing his name to what was the cause of death. And her doctor, with compassion and understanding beyond duty, did that. He wrote that death was caused by cancer. If he had promised to care for people, I was one of them. And I could never thank him. I left it all in an untidy heap until now when I sort through it and write this.

I was forty-one years old, and I was apathetic about all the purpose-created bouquets and wreath-like arrangements that arrived for me. What, I wondered, was the point? They didn't make me feel any better about what had happened, and they too would be dead soon.

One afternoon, I returned from shopping to find that someone had left a tiny bunch of wild flowers and a scribbled note on the doorstep. 'Came for a cuppa, sorry I missed you.'

Say it with flowers? She got it right, beautifully.

Late in her life, Mother had worn long knitted cardigans which announced 'I'm handmade'. A knitted belt was caught up at each side, and pockets hung down as though hands had thrust them into bag-shapes. I found this image endearing and familiar. The surprise in each humble garment was colour. An assortment of pinks and purples so bright they deafened. What she teamed with her creations was varied. On Tuesday, navy pants and the solid shoes she called her beetle-crushers. On Wednesday? Who could guess? It was these familiar outer garments of which it was hardest to let go. To give away to a charity to sell to someone else.

I was greatly relieved when the simple cremation was over. However, my biggest concern was the thought of going back to work.

On 30 December 1981, I made a long entry in my journal, and I still have the two handwritten pages. I wrote,

> Eight weeks ago, I helped my mother to die. I justified it at the time by acknowledging that, faced with the alternative, it was her wish. Ahead lay weeks of increasing pain from her cancer, debilitation, and the degrading acceptance of others doing everything for her as she grew slowly weaker. To the end, her brave veneer of cheerfulness did not crack and she never complained of her pain. She also refused, as she believed, to be made confused and sleepy by the drugs that may have alleviated it.
>
> Eight weeks ago, my actions seemed clear-cut, and easily condoned in my own mind. Since then, the burden on my conscience has increased. Is it the knowledge that I helped intentionally to end the life of another human being? Is it the going against all my study to become a nurse and to save life? Is it committing a crime in the eyes of the law? I don't truly believe it is any of these things that plague my conscience.
>
> I feel I have no one I can really talk to. My close family, while knowing what I did, gave their loving thanks that I was able to do it, and so are the only people to whom I cannot confess my feelings, and I don't want to talk at random to friends.
>
> I think my real fear is that helping someone to end their life is so easy if one has the knowledge and the ability to do it. Another fear is that I could do it again, and I could, because I believe in the dignity of death over the alternatives in a terminal and painful illness. Also, if I can do this for my own mother whom I loved so very much, could I not then, with less conscience, kill any other human being who requested it?
>
> However, as a healthy, happy, positive mother and a nurse, I also believe that life is incredibly precious.
>
> All this I have thought.
>
> No. I believe now that it was the greatest act of love I have ever been called upon to perform. I ask only that I can hold up my head the rest of my days, and try to feel humble and grateful, and most of all accepting of one small part of my life. I believe that I am very privileged.

I did think a lot about the idea of the Catholic faith. Confession interested me, but one can only confess something one regrets, and I wasn't sure about that part.

St Jude, on the other hand, patron saint of desperate causes and helper of the hopeless, with a feast day on 28 October, seemed like my sort of saint, and we had a few one-sided conversations.

Now my parents' framed wedding photograph has stood in its place for many years. Moved only occasionally when I dust the shelf, it is a familiar part of my home. How poignant to look at both your faces now with my own knowledge of a future you could never expect to see. It is akin to the comprehension that you possessed a past of your own that, despite our love, I didn't share.

Lives lead to more lives. On and on, love fulfils itself, and I know that like you, I shall never see all the future of my children. I can only hope that I too shall become a framed photograph on a shelf. That treasured possession, a familiar and loved face dusted at infrequent intervals.

*

I left work finally to enjoy grandchildren, to photograph creatures in my garden, and to continue writing. Blessed with healthy and seemingly happy grandkids, I was enchanted watching them grow and develop one generation removed.

I was also blessed with the time the two older ones spent with me and Jemma with her unconditional doggy love. They tumbled together, shared food when they thought I wasn't looking, and sometimes Jemma was a patient and contented passenger on a kitchen-chair train created across the tiled floor.

One morning, to the horror of all of us, she managed to drag a dead rat back through the dog door with her.

But, as children grow older, so do dogs.

Letters appeared in the newspapers from time to time asking why terminally ill human beings do not have a right to die at the time of their choosing. Indignant words. Angry words. Sometimes berating the medical profession as a whole for insisting that people should live and experience pain to their last agonising breath.

The sentiment that dogs can be put to sleep was a frequent argument. I wonder, though, at what mental health cost to veterinary doctors.

Now, at fifteen years of age, Jemma's old heart was failing, and she slept for more of each day. She was on diuretics, potassium supplements and, with analgesia, any restless pacing had ceased. On some days she ate little.

I considered it fortunate that, when she needed to, Jemma got to the other side of the dog door in the laundry. When raining, it was often only as far as the doormat.

My daughter on her visits saw this sweet old dog and chided me. 'Come on, Mum, dogs are lucky, there's euthanasia.'

'Yes, I know, I'll take her soon,' I heard myself say vaguely.

I didn't, though. How to choose the day or time? Which morning, which meal should be Jemma's last? I couldn't seem to make up my mind to do it.

When I saw the vet for more tablets, she validated my feelings of indecision. She said Jemma would tell me herself when she was ready to die. I was not so sure, but each morning as I stroked this beautiful dog's head and look into her clouded eyes, I searched for quality of life. It is so much easier to be passive than active and Jemma was making me think.

Being unable to make a judgement on behalf of a beloved dog. I began to wonder whether euthanasia for humanity was really going to be an easy tool.

Soon, the time did come to say goodbye to Jemma.

I woke on Thursday to a dark, rainy morning, and Jemma was lying on her bed. She opened her eyes and tried to get up, but her legs gave way. I took her some breakfast but she ate nothing. That's when I knew Jemma wasn't well, and I took her in the car to the vet.

She listened to Jemma's heart with a stethoscope, and told me that our lovely girl was just very old and would die soon. 'Take her home, keep her warm, give her anything she wants to eat, and bring her back tomorrow,' she said.

Jemma and I had a lovely afternoon and evening together. I cooked steak for her dinner and she ate it all up. I stroked her and told her how much we all loved her, and said thank-you for being a true friend. She fell asleep and when I got up a few times in the night to see if she was okay, she was snoring softly. That made me happy.

Next morning, I made chicken sandwiches for Jemma and she loved them but we had to go back to the vet at one o'clock. I helped Jemma into the car and we drove slowly up the road to the clinic. Our vet let Jemma rest in a quiet room, and I sat with her and stroked her as she fell asleep. Soon, the doctor vet came in and listened to her heart again. Our beautiful Jemma had died.

I wrote that for my grandchildren.

When I woke on that Thursday morning, Jemma's bed was full of blood. Distressed, I rang the clinic and took Jemma in. She was bleeding from a malignant tumour on her abdomen. The vet and I agreed it was time to put her to sleep. We cried.

'Tomorrow. Bring her back tomorrow at one o'clock,' and I stumbled out with the dear half blind, deaf old bull terrier bitch.

Home was our sanctuary, and we spent the next twenty-four hours as I wrote for the kids, but I watched the time. As our one o'clock appointment drew near the next day, I helped Jemma into the back of the car. We did drive slowly up the road, but I went twice past the clinic to detour around the streets in the winter sunshine before I could bring myself to drive into the car park. Our vet was waiting for us.

I wasn't devastated that Jemma's long life was to end; she could have gone on no longer. I was distressed that the gentle, dignified old girl was overpowered by human beings intent on her death. I held her lovely head as she tried so hard to resist, but soon her doctor got into a vein. 'Oh, well done, good girl,' I whispered, but whether to her, or to Jemma I wasn't sure. It didn't take long. Jemma looked beautiful in death, with her nose between her paws on the linoleum floor.

Goodbye, lovely lady.

Often, we choose not to tell small children whom we love and protect that we will allow the veterinarian to kill our pet. Maybe we should be honest. Prepare them for the realities of life ahead?

*

My letters to *youdeadnow* began after a conversation I had with myself when the youngest of the three, a girl, became eleven years old. I remembered what happened one afternoon as I travelled home from school at the same age.

'I want to wrap her in cotton wool.'

'That's a cliché.'

'I don't care. It's a great concept.'

'Yes. A lovely thought.'

'Anyway, I've started doing something for me. I've begun to write letters. Letters to a man. I call him *youdeadnow*, all lower case.'

My first letters were raw. I allowed myself to have words for what had happened. An adult vocabulary full of expletives and condemnation.

I had no words at eleven to get the whole horrible incident scribbled onto paper. Now, I gave myself permission to do so.

The letters poured onto the pages. Hesitant at first, then flowing without difficulty.

youdeadnow. And yes you are because I was eleven years old, and you were a man then. You, were a 'grown-up'.

I'm on the train. Going home. In a corner seat, in my school uniform, I'm looking out of the window and thinking about my homework.

But, *youdeadnow*, you're there too. A man in a raincoat on a suburban train. But you are not looking out of your window. You are looking at me.

You poor pathetic bastard. Sex with yourself, watching the increasing shock and confusion on a little girl's face. I didn't know what you were doing, only that you were looking at me. Challenging me to be part of it. Did you do that only once? Or was it every afternoon?

youdeadnow. It wasn't anything to do with me being there, returning from school that afternoon, was it? Any small girl in school uniform could have been your prey. That is my distressing observation.

youdeadnow. You didn't bend the rules. You broke not only the law of the courts, but also that of living as a human being upon this earth.

However, if that is the nearest to intimacy that you have known, I'm sad for you.

I believe now that you were probably more damaged before that afternoon than I was afterwards. When you were a two-year-old trying to make sense of your world, was it a sad world? Were you hurt? Were you abused?

It's not for me to forgive you, but to put it aside and let you be. An impoverished man and dead now.

I realised that every letter I wrote made something that had interrupted nights over my lifetime with occasional dark memories become of little importance. I was humbled by seeing for the first time the miserable lonely person he must have been, and let the past rest in peace scribbled on a few sheets of paper.

As the train drew into my station, I opened the carriage door. I almost fell onto the platform, and I walked home. I never told anyone, because, simply, I didn't have the words to do so.

I wonder who cared for him later. Did that man's life end in a nursing home? If he had been admitted into my care, I hope my professional work would always have been without making judgement. I imagine I would have got him safely onto the bus with all the others.

And he may, at weekends, have heard me singing.

*

Writer Paul Arden, born in England in 1940, wrote the interesting premise, 'It's better to regret what you have done than what you haven't.'

With the wish that *youdeadnow* went to wherever it is we go with a few regrets, I began to consider another concept. A packing problem Most of us have packed a suitcase or a small bag to go on a journey somewhere. To hospital to have a baby? A simple picnic? Or maybe for a long-awaited holiday. But to pack a suitcase for the last journey of all? The hand luggage, crammed full or almost empty, with which to arrive in heaven?

I have tossed the idea around, not only in my own head, but with others.

I think for me it would be a host of A4 notepads and a pen that never ran out of ink.

A young man said he would pack his fears. Over drinks at the pub, someone stated that what he would not want to find in his suitcase was his ex-wife, and another asked, 'How many bottles of brandy fit into a suitcase anyway?'

A few favourite books would be nice, and also music. Maybe Vera Lynn's 'Faraway Places', or better still, 'Wish me luck as you wave me goodbye'.

A handyman said, 'All my tools of course. There may be a few odd jobs that need doing up there.'

One teenager said, 'Maybe a Bible would earn me points for getting good accommodation,' while her friend shrugged and suggested travelling light and hoping for the best.

I suppose that, as when there is danger of a house fire, beloved photographs would be an obvious first thought. And every one of the good memories. Pack them in. All the fabric of a life that has made us what we are.

To arrive in heaven with a case full of regrets would be sad, but maybe even that is better than nothing at all.

This ultimate journey? Of course the suitcase is a figurative one. But for what, I wonder, in this real world of ours.

Maybe best of all to take with us is the belief in both freedom from all worries, and complete peace.

Have I helped anyone pack theirs? I hope so.

One thing I have done is to assist children pack for their first school camp. On one occasion to drop a small child at the bus and return home to find the warm jacket, on its way to being included, thrown over the back of a kitchen chair.

Apart from following the excursion bus to camp like an overprotective parent, one can only sigh at lack of vigilance. It's not life-threatening. More life-teaching, and it will probably never happen again.

*

And this is where the cricket in my house reminds me about the end of my father's life.

Dad was very lonely without our mother and after several years agreed to come to Perth. It was two months after his eighty-third birthday. One of my sisters brought him across Australia to live with me and my family because he needed daily care. Living on his own, he was forgetting to turn off the gas cooker after preparing a meal. He was drinking a few glasses of sherry instead of eating the meal he had just put on the table and his granddad flat was waiting for him when the time came. The sunny little flat with its small kitchenette overlooked the rear garden with a lovely pergola and a pool, and Jemma was still the family pet.

I was halfway through my forties and working part-time. Some evenings, I helped Dad with his bottle of sherry into my old Volvo, and drove to a nearby riverside café. There, I parked overlooking the water, bought him a pie or a sausage roll, and poured him a drink in a plastic glass. He sat contentedly in the car watching people pass by and the occasional sailboat, while I took our beloved Jemma for a walk. Cocktails on the Swan River. My way. Simple pleasure for both of us, and how much I value the memory.

On one of those evenings, as we approached the car after her walk, the dog rolled over and over on a couple of dead fish.

'How lovely,' she showed me in dog language, her tail almost out of control.

'How disgusting,' I told her in English.

And how, I wondered, was I going to get the smelly bitch home. Then I remembered that the car boot was empty. Hoping no one was watching, I managed to lift Jemma at arm's length, stow her carefully in, and close the lid. How many minutes of air for twenty-five kilos of dog? It was only a short journey and I did hope it was not an evening when at a stop sign, someone asked me politely for directions. With relief, I pulled into my driveway and wondered whom to help out first. Dad waited patiently in the front passenger seat.

I pushed him too, in a cheap wheelchair bought from a neighbour, my arms outstretched, my legs making our journey happen on riverside paths that I had thought looked completely flat. It was an effective means of transportation not built for much comfort, and it lived, folded up, outside the front door.

One morning, the wheelchair was missing, the two metal armrests thrown onto the lawn. I phoned the local police station.

'Yes,' stated a male voice, 'an article of that description has been recovered in your suburb. Probably young people skylarking. Seems to be happening a lot. We have it here, but I have to ask, madam, was there anyone in the wheelchair when it was removed from your property?'

Little birthday cake candles come in packets of twelve, and buying seven of them for Dad's cake the next year was easy. We sat around him in the garden, and on a six-inch-square lamington I lit the eighty-four candles. It was a bonfire. Dad, in his red birthday braces, was an image that stays in my mind. His face creased up with uncontrollable laughter at that wonderful moment in his life.

And that moment I do have captured for ever as a photograph.

The extinguished cake covered in candle wax was no longer fit to eat.

My father was slowly ending his life at one end of the house. Young adult kids were energetically living their lives at the other end. It was a big house. I wandered through rooms. I drifted between places and embraced the spaces in between, where I tried to find myself, often with a glass of wine in my hand.

I watched half a movie on television with the husband I no longer have, and thought of my father, my beloved father alone, waiting till it was time for bed. I wandered down to sit with him thinking this was a crazy way to live. Now, as more and more my own life moves on, I understand his clock-watching loneliness, but never did he plead, 'Stay a little longer, my dear.'

Dad loved Jemma-dog. He enjoyed her company and I encouraged her to visit his granddad flat on many evenings too.

'Up on the chair,' he'd say, and she was happy to do so.

They dozed in separate armchairs whiling time away. Sometimes, I took my paints and my watercolour dreams and silently worked in a corner of his room as he quietly talked of life. Some special moments, but it was at about that time that our roles began to change.

One morning, he cheerfully told me that he had forgotten to take his little blue heart tablet for a few days and had just taken three or maybe it was four to make up for that.

I began to be a little more vigilant in supervision of medications.

Dad began to require help with his morning shower, and other basic hygiene needs. Ordinary life skills with which a mother assists a child, and I called my new child Rupert. My father embraced his new name with amusement. It became a pet name, and for some of the things I had to help him with, I found it an easier term to use than 'Dad'.

I wondered how it would feel to see my own father naked for the first time. Confronting? Wrong word. Embarrassing? No. It was simply a little strange, and then not strange at all. Just another human being requiring a bit of help with things along the way.

Rupert and the lost pyjamas reads like a very slightly adult-rated children's story. Every evening, I walked our dog for her visit to the back lawn before bed. On one of those trips, through the window, I saw Rupert standing in his room completely naked. On return to the house, I decided to make sure he was all right.

'Can't find my pyjamas,' he said in answer to my question.

'Okay,' I said as one does when children mislay their belongings, 'where did you last see them?'

'I'm not sure.'

Oh well. At least that sounded honest. I surveyed the floor, peered under the bed, lifted pillows. No pyjamas. And then I really went on a hunt for those necessary items, and, because my search was thorough, I found them. In the microwave oven.

Of course.

After that, as I handed them over, the bitch within me said, 'We don't usually stand completely naked in the kitchen.'

And I received the perfect response. 'It's my kitchen.'

Joyce Grenfell, born in 1910 and one of England's best loved entertainers in her time, wrote,

> If I should die before the rest of you,
> Break not a flower nor inscribe a stone
> Nor, when I'm gone, speak in a Sunday voice,
> But be the usual selves that I have known,
> Weep if you must.
> Parting is hell.
> But life goes on,
> So…sing as well

Our mother left those words, for all of us, her family to find and to read after she had died.

Late one night, I heard Rupert singing quietly in his room. I put my hand out to turn the door handle and go in but hesitated, wondering which would be worse. Singing sadly in your room instead of weeping, or learning that someone could hear you? That night, I left him to be alone.

On 3 November 1989, the day before the eight-year anniversary of Mother's death, he asked me to buy him a bottle of brandy.

We both knew he still had a large bottle of barbiturates in the drawer beside his bed.

I wondered if he might be thinking of taking them that night, wanting not to be alive the next morning, and mentally prepared myself for the possibility.

It didn't happen.

*

I took over more vigilant care, but just over four months later, Rupert fell in his room early one morning and my son heard him calling out. We helped him onto his bed, his doctor visited, gave him pain relief for a suspected fractured knee, and phoned for an ambulance.

As I waited with Rupert, he said sadly, 'We were doing so well, weren't we, my dear?'

I look back now and reflect on the three years that this kindly and undemanding son of an Anzac and I lived once again under the same roof. The Rupert years. A heart-warming time.

I did on occasions feel irritation at the inability to make a spontaneous decision to stay in town for dinner. I had sighed sometimes at my increasing obligations to his well-being. But, within considerations like those, as a family had we loved him enough?

Did I hug him with words while I still had the chance?

He was transferred to a small hospital staffed by Catholic nursing nuns. He had no choice. Brought up by a mother who thought the Catholic faith was not to be recommended, they were so kind and skilled that he soon learned to appreciate, if not love, them. He was to remain there for eight weeks and I wished he could be nursed there for ever. If I could not fulfil my wish for him to die in his own bed, he was in a good place.

Rupert was respected by the staff who looked after him. I believe too that he raised a bit of a smile at times. He told the Reverend Mother when she visited him that she should jolly well practise active euthanasia in her precious hospital. I was there too, and across the bed her eyes met mine with understanding and pity.

Maybe also not such a good idea was to inform the priest who visited the following afternoon that he was having a 'hell of a day', but I expect the priest had heard worse. Possibly he wished he could echo the sentiment.

His orthopaedic surgeon was informed that his theatre was a shambles and that the X-ray staff had no idea how to run their department. All that was relayed to me by amused staff.

After that, Rupert settled in but became more muddled as the days went on. On one visit, he solemnly delighted me with an incredible story about the equidistant rabbits that had come to see him the previous evening.

Next day, he asked me, 'Do you remember when you came home from school and you were angry because I had eaten all the oranges?'

I tried hard to do so, till I realised he thought I was his older brother. What a perfect bit of confusion, going back about eighty years. I wish now that I had gone back there with him more often, instead of repeatedly trying to bring him back to our present time together.

However, as we continued on this journey, while he still often thought he was talking with his brother, he sometimes appeared to believe that I was the Virgin Mary.

His time there ran out.

Admitted to long-term care in a nursing home within walking distance from my family home, he shared a room with three other men. I don't believe any of them ever spoke to each other. All appeared either confused, or isolated in the disappointment and abject misery of this final residence. Rupert too became very depressed. On one early visit, I found him glaring silently at the foil-wrapped Easter egg on his breakfast tray.

He also began to deteriorate physically. The physiotherapist who visited asked what were my expectations, and sadly we agreed that there was little that would help now. He was lifted out of bed each morning and spent his days in a wheelchair.

'They're keeping me alive here with legs that don't work any more,' he told me unhappily. He expressed a wish to contract bronchopneumonia to help him leave the world. A bit like waiting at a bus stop for a service suspended for a while.

Each day when I visited, he said, 'Just bring me, please my dear, everything out of the top drawer by my bed.'

And I knew what he wanted. The pills he had left it too late to take. But to bring them into a nursing home? I could have tipped the whole contents of the drawer into a bag and taken it to him but it could all go wrong and inevitably I would be implicated. So my answer every day was always the same.

I visited two or three times each day for ten weeks. Some friends told me it was excessive and unnecessary, but for me it was a need. He was my child, unhappy in an unfamiliar place, but fortunately without any pain.

Eventually, over a few pitiable days, I became aware that it was not to be for much longer, and I left one evening to go home and sleep but with the request that I wished to be with my father when he died.

*

The phone call wasn't unexpected. My clothes were laid out ready, and I returned to the nursing home late in the same night. The staff were thoughtful, found me a chair and a rug to sit beside Rupert's bed and pulled the curtains around it. These, I could tell, were to be his last few hours, and I told him quietly that I was close by. I was with him.

'Thank you,' he whispered. Briefly, he lifted his hand from where it lay on the bedcover, and turned it palm upward, spreading his fingers. A gesture encompassing this last night together, as he said his final words. 'I'm all right, my dear,' and he paused. 'I'm all right.'

Hopefully, in a perfect world, we may all have someone to whom we can say this as, aware of our final moments, we prepare to die.

As the hours passed, so did the winter solstice. Friday had become Saturday. I poured sherry for myself into a plastic tumbler, from the almost empty bottle in the little cupboard by the bed, and a nurse brought me another rug. No more words passed between Rupert and me, and his breathing, which was shallow, became more so over the hours.

To be with someone who is dying is an awesome experience. To accept the inevitable on their behalf.

I had plenty of time to think back over the last ten weeks. I remembered that there had been good days.

On one Sunday afternoon visit, I found Rupert sitting in his wheelchair, out in the sunshine with other residents. He had a bright crocheted rug over his thin knees, a glass of sherry in his hand, and a broad smile on his face.

One of the carers said to me, 'What a pity you don't have a camera.'

'But I do,' I remembered, and rummaged through my bag. The photograph I took that day is still among my treasures.

When I visit next day, Rupert asks me, 'Are the children I've been playing with all day dying too? Or is it just me?'

Now I can only keep watch. There is no more to do. Nothing to busy myself with. Are you aware? Do you know I still perch awkwardly on this wooden chair some busy person dragged here hours ago? To be with you now is my privilege.

For the last time, I stroke your hand. I touch your face. The coldness only validates my knowledge that you are dying. So I wait, staring at my thoughts.

Roger Whittaker invades my head. 'For you are beautiful, and I have loved you dearly, more dearly than the spoken word can tell', and I almost smile, because, for me, Elvis did it better.

The last farewell. My heart is full of tears…

My beloved Daddy, Dad, my father and now Rupert, in the full circle of life, a child again.

You take a shallow shuddering breath and claim my nearness one last time, and then it is over.

Eventually, I stand. Knowing. Seconds tick, tick, tick by. Minutes pass, and I walk quietly away trusting others to watch over you.

Suitcase packed and on the bus.

Rupert had finally died a few minutes after seven in the morning. He had waited for his beloved day staff to come on duty. The team who had worked hard each day to keep him comfortable, and as happy as was possible.

My father, my beloved Rupert, had done it the slow way. Travelled the last part of his journey cared for by others, but for a mercifully short time.

Each time he had asked me to bring him the tablets by his bed at my home, I had said, 'I can't.'

I believe it was the only thing I ever refused to do for him, and it breaks my heart to write those two words now.

Goodbye, little crickety-thing, small creature who came to end your life in my home. Thank you for these many diverse memories. I have learned that crickets are considered to be lucky, and I feel honoured to have had you in my life. Also, I find myself wondering what you might have put into your little suitcase before you finally died and I buried you in my garden with a vivid nasturtium flower.

The cricket sang,
And set the sun,…
… And so the night became.

Emily Dickinson (1830–1886)

www.ingramcontent.com/pod-product-compliance
Lightning Source LLC
Chambersburg PA
CBHW062155100526
44589CB00014B/1845